as in fox

This colourful book covers
the twenty six letters of the alphabet.
Each letter is illustrated
with a bold picture and the name of this object
is printed clearly underneath.
The objects all begin with the *sound*
of each letter, except 'x', rather than the *name*
of the letter (i.e. 'a' for apple not 'a' for able)
making this book invaluable for young children
before they can read.

Available in Series S808

* **a is for apple**
* **I can count**
Tell me the time
Colours and shapes
* **Nursery Rhymes**

**Also available as* Ladybird Teaching Friezes

Published by Ladybird Books Ltd Loughborough Leicestershire UK
Ladybird Books Inc Lewiston Maine 04240 USA
© LADYBIRD BOOKS LTD MCMLXXX

a is for apple

illustrated by LYNN N. GRUNDY

Ladybird Books

apple

b

ball

c

cat

d

duck

elephant

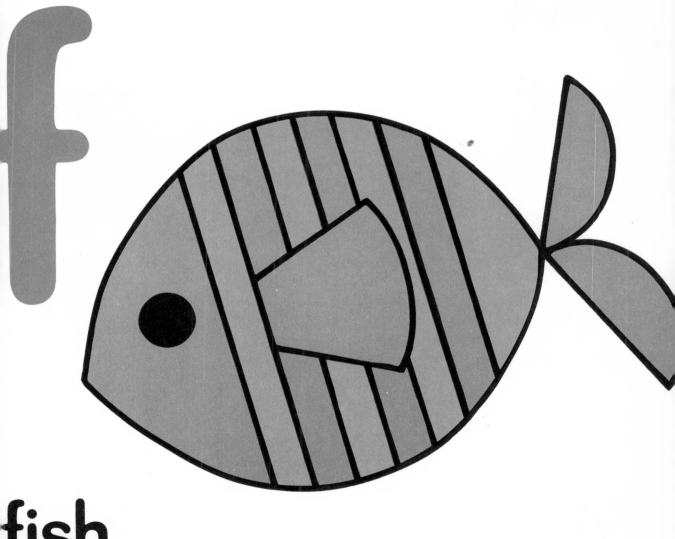

f

fish

g

goat

h

house

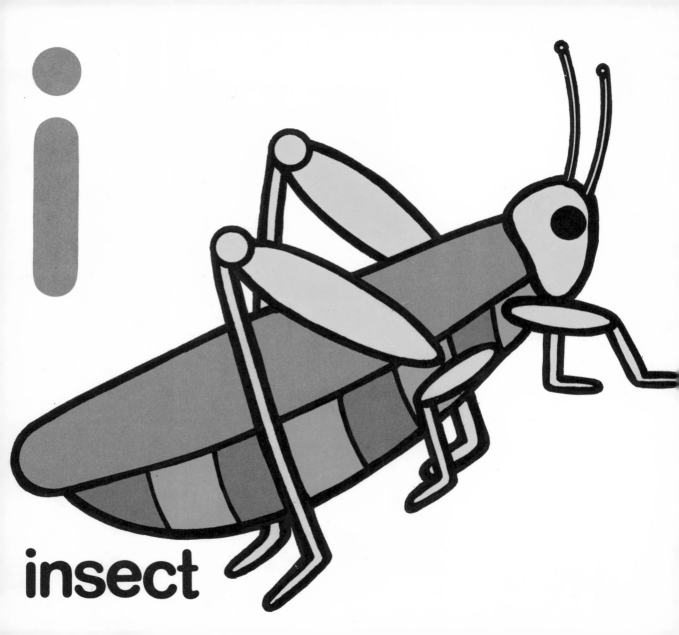

i

insect

j

jam

k

kangaroo

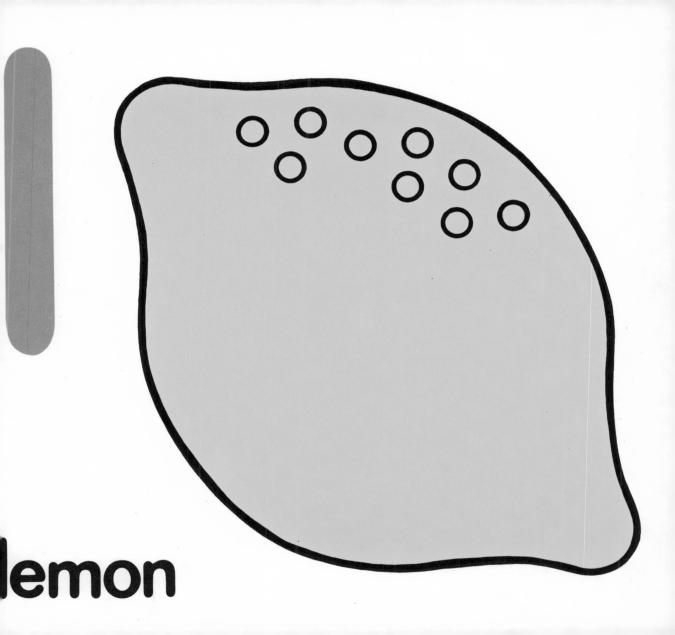

lemon

m

mouse

n

nurse

octopus

panda

q

queen

r

rabbit

S

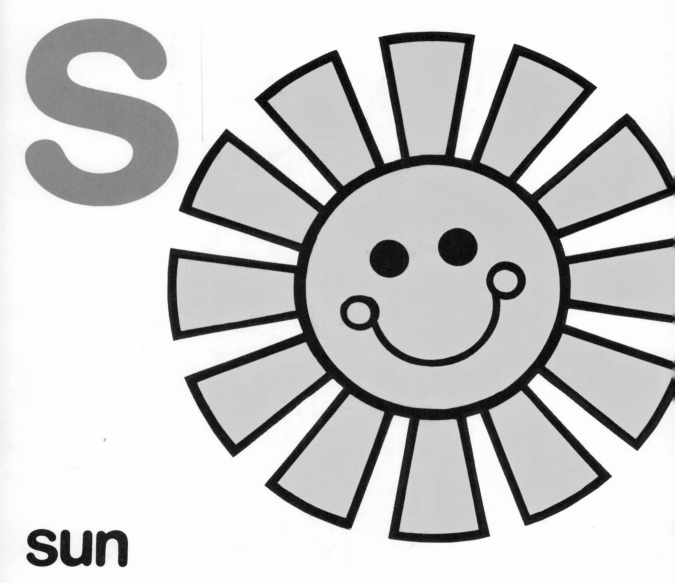

sun

t

television

u

umbrella

violin

watch

x as in fox

y

yacht